Let's Take a Trip

A Mountain Adventure

by Patricia Griffith Morgan

photography by Michael Plunkett and Tom Herde

Troll Associates

Library of Congress Cataloging in Publication Data

Morgan, Patricia Griffith.
    A mountain adventure.

    (Let's take a trip)
    Summary: Follows a group of hikers as they climb
Mount Katahdin, highest peak in Maine, observing the
flora, fauna, and sights of interest along the way.
        1. Hiking—Maine—Juvenile literature.
[1. Katahdin, Mount (Me.) 2. Hiking. 3. Mountains]
I. Plunkett, Michael, ill.   II. Herde, Tom, ill.
III. Title.
GV199.42.M2M67   1988   917.41   87-3486
ISBN 0-8167-1173-9 (lib. bdg.)
ISBN 0-8167-1174-7 (pbk.)

The author and publisher wish to thank Chris Drew of Baxter State Park for his assistance, and to acknowledge
Craig Blouin for the photographs on pages 5,6,7, and 12-19.

Mount Katahdin is a mile-high mountain and the highest peak in Maine! It was named by the Abnaki Indians, who once lived in its forests. *Katahdin* means "greatest mountain," and to many that's just what it is! Hundreds of hikers face the challenge of climbing Katahdin each year. Let's follow some hikers to the top.

Katahdin is part of Baxter State Park, which contains many forests and streams. Everyone who visits the park must register at the ranger stations. Rangers keep records of all the hikers in case of emergencies. Did someone wander off a trail? Is a group caught in a rainstorm? The rangers must know exactly how many hikers may need their help.

After registering, the group heads for
Katahdin Stream Campground, where they
will spend the night. The campground has
covered picnic areas, tent sites, bunkhouses
and *lean-tos*. The lean-tos, or three-sided sheds,
protect campers from wind or rainy weather. Fires
in metal drums keep campers warm on cold,
windy nights.

One of the hikers is getting her gear together
for the climb the next day. She carefully places
a first-aid kit near the top of her backpack. It
may come in handy for insect bites, scrapes,
twisted ankles—or even blisters caused by new
hiking boots!

In the early morning light, the hikers decide which trail to take to the top. They are eager to meet the challenge of climbing Mount Katahdin. An early start is important in order to have enough time for the climb. They must get to the top and back down again before darkness sets in.

The adventurers first pass a meadow where a big bull moose is taking a stroll. The long flap of skin that hangs down from his neck is known as the moose's *bell*. A large male moose is up to nine feet long and as much as seven feet high. It can weigh over one thousand pounds.

The hikers soon reach Katahdin Falls and the
bridge crossing Katahdin Stream. The tall
pine and spruce trees are powdered with snow.
But soon there will be no trees. More than
halfway up the mountain the hikers will reach
the *timber line*. Beyond this line, there is rock
instead of soil and winds can be of hurricane
force. Trees cannot survive conditions beyond the
timber line.

The trail up the mountain is part of the much longer *Appalachian Trail*. The Appalachian Trail begins in Georgia and passes through fourteen states, two national parks, and eight national forests! It ends at the top of Mount Katahdin at a place called *Baxter Peak*.

The trail is marked all along its length with white *blazes* that are used as landmarks. The blazes help keep hikers on track—if they *don't* see a blaze after a distance, they may very well be lost! The blazes are made by stripping a small piece of bark from a tree with an ax. The patch is then painted white so it can be seen easily.

Further along the trail is a *stand,* or place where new trees are growing. No one knows exactly what killed the taller, dead trees in the background. It could have been a forest fire, or maybe some disease. Or very strong winds might have broken off tree tops and stripped the bark so they had no protection.

The hikers rest and look toward their destination—Baxter Peak! It still seems so far away! The hikers have just reached the timber line. Some trees are still trying to grow, but most have given in to the wind and weather. Now they grow together for protection in low mats of cedar, spruce, and pine. These clusters of trees are called *krummholz*.

The trail winds over a rocky plain that looks somewhat like a moonscape. Another group of hikers has built a *cairn,* or pile of rocks, to mark the trail. The climb gets steeper. Hikers must squeeze through a narrow crevice of rock! The hikers must be in very good shape to climb to the top of Katahdin!

No, they're not on top of the mountain yet—
this is one of the smaller peaks on the way.
Still, it feels good to have made it this far. It's
like being on top of the world! The hikers spot
lichens (LIKE-ens) growing on the rocks. Lichens
are the only form of plant life that exists this high
up on the mountain.

One of the climbers stops to rest and to take a drink of water. Mountain climbing is very hard work, and the body loses moisture by sweating. That's why it is very important to have water nearby at all times! The hikers relax at *Thoreau Spring,* named after the writer, Henry David Thoreau.

They're almost at the top, but first they must climb a jagged edge of rock. The sharp, rocky surface is called *Knife Edge*. Can you see how it got its name? Knife Edge is the toughest part of the climb, but most of the hikers have made it. The others push on. They know that Baxter Peak is not too far away!

Success! They've made it to the top—elevation 5,267 feet! That's just about a mile! Years ago, some climbers built a cairn on top of Baxter Peak. The cairn brought the elevation of the peak up to exactly one mile. Can you figure out how many feet the cairn had to be in order to do this?

After enjoying the view and resting awhile, the hikers start back down Katahdin. They can see many ponds in the park below. On the mountain they must watch their footing. Loose rock can turn beneath their feet—the climb down the mountain is tricky! Again, the hikers see patches of krummholz. The timber line is still below them.

Another group of hikers is on its way down the mountain. Two have stopped at the timber line to inspect a tiny, dwarfed evergreen. Others are all the way down the trail and are walking through a forest. What a beautiful day for a hike!

Signs point the way to various trails. Some hikers visit Basin Pond. The sign reminds them that they may not camp there; they may camp only where rangers are stationed! This is for the campers' protection so that rangers can keep track of them.

Basin Pond is a circle lake, also known as a
cirque. It was formed when the last glacier, or
huge mass of ice, retreated from Maine some
12,000 years ago. Many large rocks were
embedded underneath the glacier. As the glacier
moved, the rocks dug up the ground that was
underneath. It formed a shallow basin where
water later collected.

It's time to move on to Chimney Pond Campground. The hikers check their guidebook to be sure they are on the right trail. At last, they arrive! After a day of hiking, the bunkhouse is a welcome sight. The group will stay here overnight and finish the trip in the morning.

Chimney Pond is what is known as a "carry-in, carry-out" campground. This means that hikers must bring supplies with them and then carry them away. Since open fires are not allowed, portable gas stoves are used for cooking. An open fire, caught by strong winds, can start a forest fire!

A camper relaxes beside Chimney Pond and looks out at the Knife Edge. Perhaps he's marveling at the fact that he made it across that sharp ridge of rock! It's been a long day, and just looking around provides a nice change of pace.

Others explore Baxter State Park to get a closer look at the ponds. A mixed forest of evergreens and hardwood trees—maple, beech, and birch—forms a beautiful background for one pond. One lowland area, where water has gathered, is slowly becoming a marsh.

Bridges built of planks or logs cross most of
the small streams and marshes. But one hiker
finds a stream he must cross by hopping on
stepping-stones! Another hiker relaxes beside
a beautiful waterfall.

A group of young hikers tries to decide where they will go from here. Others follow a nature trail. It leads them through a *bog*. The soft, wet ground is often springy with moss-like matter called *peat*. Many low bushes that flower in the spring—blueberry, elderberry, Labrador Tea— can be found along the trail.

After a day of exploring the trails, the hikers look forward to resting. Daicey Pond Campground has cabins, which are more comfortable than bunkhouses. One young man holds up a bit of food to attract a Canada jay. The wild bird, who has spotted the food, actually lands on his hand!

The hikers need plenty of firewood for this cold fall night in the woods. One smart camper carries wood back to camp the easy way—by canoe! Canoes can be rented at Daicey Pond to fish or enjoy the water! At the end of the day, canoeists head back to the dock and then back to camp.

One camper hopes there's still enough time to
catch a fish for dinner. Sunapee trout and
blueback charr, which is like salmon, are
abundant in Daicey Pond.

As the sun sets behind the mountain, Katahdin takes on a reddish glow. Many will leave in the morning as the new groups of hikers arrive. Perhaps someday you will meet the challenge of climbing the "greatest mountain."